THIS BOOK BELONGS TO:

CONTACT INFORMATION	
NAME:	
ADDRESS:	
PHONE:	

START / END DATES

/ / TO / /

DEDICATION

This Cabin Guest Book is dedicated to all the people out there who want to record their guests and document their findings in the process.

You are my inspiration for producing books and I'm honored to be a part of keeping all of your Cabin Guest Book notes and records organized.

This journal notebook will help you record the details of guests' stay.

Thoughtfully put together with these sections to record: Guest Name, Date Arrived, Traveling From, Contact, Date Departed, Favorite Things About The Cabin, Places I Recommend, Favorite Memory, and Message To The Host.

HOW TO USE THIS BOOK

The purpose of this book is to keep all of your Cabin Guest Book notes all in one place. It will help keep you organized.

This Cabin Guest Book will allow you to accurately document details about your Guests' Stay.

Here are examples of the prompts for you to fill in and write about your experience in this book:

1. Guest Name - Names of your visitors.
2. Date Arrived - Dates of their arrival.
3. Traveling From - Where did they travel from.
4. Contact - Write their address, email, phone number.
5. Date Departed - Dates of their departure.
6. Favorite Things About The Cabin - Space for them to write what they liked best about the cabin.
7. Places I Would Recommend - Your guests can write their recommendations such as restaurants, shopping, entertainment, etc.
8. Favorite Memory From Your Stay - A place for your guests to write their favorite memory.
9. Message To The Host - Blank lined notes for them to leave a comment or message for the host.

CABIN GUEST

GUEST NAME		CONTACT NUMBER	
DATE ARRIVED		DATE DEPARTED	
TRAVELING FROM			

FAVORITE THING ABOUT THE CABIN

PLACES I WOULD RECOMMEND (RESTAURANTS, SHOPPING, ENTERTAINMENT, ETC.)

FAVORITE MEMORY FROM YOUR STAY	MESSAGE TO THE HOST

CABIN GUEST

GUEST NAME		CONTACT NUMBER	
DATE ARRIVED		DATE DEPARTED	
TRAVELING FROM			

FAVORITE THING ABOUT THE CABIN

PLACES I WOULD RECOMMEND (RESTAURANTS, SHOPPING, ENTERTAINMENT, ETC.)

FAVORITE MEMORY FROM YOUR STAY	MESSAGE TO THE HOST

CABIN GUEST

GUEST NAME		CONTACT NUMBER	
DATE ARRIVED		DATE DEPARTED	
TRAVELING FROM			

FAVORITE THING ABOUT THE CABIN

PLACES I WOULD RECOMMEND
(RESTAURANTS, SHOPPING, ENTERTAINMENT, ETC.)

FAVORITE MEMORY FROM YOUR STAY	MESSAGE TO THE HOST

CABIN GUEST

GUEST NAME		CONTACT NUMBER	
DATE ARRIVED		DATE DEPARTED	
TRAVELING FROM			

FAVORITE THING ABOUT THE CABIN

PLACES I WOULD RECOMMEND
(RESTAURANTS, SHOPPING, ENTERTAINMENT, ETC.)

FAVORITE MEMORY FROM YOUR STAY	MESSAGE TO THE HOST

CABIN GUEST

GUEST NAME		CONTACT NUMBER	
DATE ARRIVED		DATE DEPARTED	
TRAVELING FROM			

FAVORITE THING ABOUT THE CABIN

PLACES I WOULD RECOMMEND (RESTAURANTS, SHOPPING, ENTERTAINMENT, ETC.)

FAVORITE MEMORY FROM YOUR STAY	MESSAGE TO THE HOST

CABIN GUEST

GUEST NAME		CONTACT NUMBER	
DATE ARRIVED		DATE DEPARTED	
TRAVELING FROM			

FAVORITE THING ABOUT THE CABIN

PLACES I WOULD RECOMMEND
(RESTAURANTS, SHOPPING, ENTERTAINMENT, ETC.)

FAVORITE MEMORY FROM YOUR STAY	MESSAGE TO THE HOST

CABIN GUEST

GUEST NAME		CONTACT NUMBER	
DATE ARRIVED		DATE DEPARTED	
TRAVELING FROM			

FAVORITE THING ABOUT THE CABIN

PLACES I WOULD RECOMMEND
(RESTAURANTS, SHOPPING, ENTERTAINMENT, ETC.)

FAVORITE MEMORY FROM YOUR STAY	MESSAGE TO THE HOST

CABIN GUEST

GUEST NAME		CONTACT NUMBER	
DATE ARRIVED		DATE DEPARTED	
TRAVELING FROM			

FAVORITE THING ABOUT THE CABIN

PLACES I WOULD RECOMMEND
(RESTAURANTS, SHOPPING, ENTERTAINMENT, ETC.)

FAVORITE MEMORY FROM YOUR STAY	MESSAGE TO THE HOST

CABIN GUEST

GUEST NAME		CONTACT NUMBER	
DATE ARRIVED		DATE DEPARTED	
TRAVELING FROM			

FAVORITE THING ABOUT THE CABIN

PLACES I WOULD RECOMMEND (RESTAURANTS, SHOPPING, ENTERTAINMENT, ETC.)

FAVORITE MEMORY FROM YOUR STAY	MESSAGE TO THE HOST

CABIN GUEST

GUEST NAME		CONTACT NUMBER	
DATE ARRIVED		DATE DEPARTED	
TRAVELING FROM			

FAVORITE THING ABOUT THE CABIN

PLACES I WOULD RECOMMEND
(RESTAURANTS, SHOPPING, ENTERTAINMENT, ETC.)

FAVORITE MEMORY FROM YOUR STAY	MESSAGE TO THE HOST

CABIN GUEST

GUEST NAME		CONTACT NUMBER	
DATE ARRIVED		DATE DEPARTED	
TRAVELING FROM			

FAVORITE THING ABOUT THE CABIN

PLACES I WOULD RECOMMEND
(RESTAURANTS, SHOPPING, ENTERTAINMENT, ETC.)

FAVORITE MEMORY FROM YOUR STAY	MESSAGE TO THE HOST

CABIN GUEST

GUEST NAME		CONTACT NUMBER	
DATE ARRIVED		DATE DEPARTED	
TRAVELING FROM			

FAVORITE THING ABOUT THE CABIN

PLACES I WOULD RECOMMEND
(RESTAURANTS, SHOPPING, ENTERTAINMENT, ETC.)

FAVORITE MEMORY FROM YOUR STAY	MESSAGE TO THE HOST

CABIN GUEST

GUEST NAME		CONTACT NUMBER	
DATE ARRIVED		DATE DEPARTED	
TRAVELING FROM			

FAVORITE THING ABOUT THE CABIN

PLACES I WOULD RECOMMEND (RESTAURANTS, SHOPPING, ENTERTAINMENT, ETC.)

FAVORITE MEMORY FROM YOUR STAY	MESSAGE TO THE HOST

CABIN GUEST

GUEST NAME		CONTACT NUMBER	
DATE ARRIVED		DATE DEPARTED	
TRAVELING FROM			

FAVORITE THING ABOUT THE CABIN

PLACES I WOULD RECOMMEND
(RESTAURANTS, SHOPPING, ENTERTAINMENT, ETC.)

FAVORITE MEMORY FROM YOUR STAY	MESSAGE TO THE HOST

CABIN GUEST

GUEST NAME		CONTACT NUMBER	
DATE ARRIVED		DATE DEPARTED	
TRAVELING FROM			

FAVORITE THING ABOUT THE CABIN

PLACES I WOULD RECOMMEND
(RESTAURANTS, SHOPPING, ENTERTAINMENT, ETC.)

FAVORITE MEMORY FROM YOUR STAY	MESSAGE TO THE HOST

CABIN GUEST

GUEST NAME		CONTACT NUMBER	
DATE ARRIVED		DATE DEPARTED	
TRAVELING FROM			

FAVORITE THING ABOUT THE CABIN

PLACES I WOULD RECOMMEND
(RESTAURANTS, SHOPPING, ENTERTAINMENT, ETC.)

FAVORITE MEMORY FROM YOUR STAY	MESSAGE TO THE HOST

CABIN GUEST

GUEST NAME		CONTACT NUMBER	
DATE ARRIVED		DATE DEPARTED	
TRAVELING FROM			

FAVORITE THING ABOUT THE CABIN

PLACES I WOULD RECOMMEND
(RESTAURANTS, SHOPPING, ENTERTAINMENT, ETC.)

FAVORITE MEMORY FROM YOUR STAY	MESSAGE TO THE HOST

CABIN GUEST

GUEST NAME		CONTACT NUMBER	
DATE ARRIVED		DATE DEPARTED	
TRAVELING FROM			

FAVORITE THING ABOUT THE CABIN

PLACES I WOULD RECOMMEND (RESTAURANTS, SHOPPING, ENTERTAINMENT, ETC.)

FAVORITE MEMORY FROM YOUR STAY	MESSAGE TO THE HOST

CABIN GUEST

GUEST NAME		CONTACT NUMBER	
DATE ARRIVED		DATE DEPARTED	
TRAVELING FROM			

FAVORITE THING ABOUT THE CABIN

PLACES I WOULD RECOMMEND (RESTAURANTS, SHOPPING, ENTERTAINMENT, ETC.)

FAVORITE MEMORY FROM YOUR STAY	MESSAGE TO THE HOST

CABIN GUEST

GUEST NAME		CONTACT NUMBER	
DATE ARRIVED		DATE DEPARTED	
TRAVELING FROM			

FAVORITE THING ABOUT THE CABIN

PLACES I WOULD RECOMMEND
(RESTAURANTS, SHOPPING, ENTERTAINMENT, ETC.)

FAVORITE MEMORY FROM YOUR STAY	MESSAGE TO THE HOST

CABIN GUEST

GUEST NAME		CONTACT NUMBER	
DATE ARRIVED		DATE DEPARTED	
TRAVELING FROM			

FAVORITE THING ABOUT THE CABIN

PLACES I WOULD RECOMMEND (RESTAURANTS, SHOPPING, ENTERTAINMENT, ETC.)

FAVORITE MEMORY FROM YOUR STAY	MESSAGE TO THE HOST

CABIN GUEST

GUEST NAME		CONTACT NUMBER	
DATE ARRIVED		DATE DEPARTED	
TRAVELING FROM			

FAVORITE THING ABOUT THE CABIN

PLACES I WOULD RECOMMEND
(RESTAURANTS, SHOPPING, ENTERTAINMENT, ETC.)

FAVORITE MEMORY FROM YOUR STAY	MESSAGE TO THE HOST

CABIN GUEST

GUEST NAME		CONTACT NUMBER	
DATE ARRIVED		DATE DEPARTED	
TRAVELING FROM			

FAVORITE THING ABOUT THE CABIN

PLACES I WOULD RECOMMEND
(RESTAURANTS, SHOPPING, ENTERTAINMENT, ETC.)

FAVORITE MEMORY FROM YOUR STAY	MESSAGE TO THE HOST

CABIN GUEST

GUEST NAME		CONTACT NUMBER	
DATE ARRIVED		DATE DEPARTED	
TRAVELING FROM			

FAVORITE THING ABOUT THE CABIN

PLACES I WOULD RECOMMEND
(RESTAURANTS, SHOPPING, ENTERTAINMENT, ETC.)

FAVORITE MEMORY FROM YOUR STAY	MESSAGE TO THE HOST

CABIN GUEST

GUEST NAME		CONTACT NUMBER	
DATE ARRIVED		DATE DEPARTED	
TRAVELING FROM			

FAVORITE THING ABOUT THE CABIN

PLACES I WOULD RECOMMEND (RESTAURANTS, SHOPPING, ENTERTAINMENT, ETC.)

FAVORITE MEMORY FROM YOUR STAY	MESSAGE TO THE HOST

CABIN GUEST

GUEST NAME		CONTACT NUMBER	
DATE ARRIVED		DATE DEPARTED	
TRAVELING FROM			

FAVORITE THING ABOUT THE CABIN

PLACES I WOULD RECOMMEND
(RESTAURANTS, SHOPPING, ENTERTAINMENT, ETC.)

FAVORITE MEMORY FROM YOUR STAY	MESSAGE TO THE HOST

CABIN GUEST

GUEST NAME		CONTACT NUMBER	
DATE ARRIVED		DATE DEPARTED	
TRAVELING FROM			

FAVORITE THING ABOUT THE CABIN

PLACES I WOULD RECOMMEND
(RESTAURANTS, SHOPPING, ENTERTAINMENT, ETC.)

FAVORITE MEMORY FROM YOUR STAY	MESSAGE TO THE HOST

CABIN GUEST

GUEST NAME		CONTACT NUMBER	
DATE ARRIVED		DATE DEPARTED	
TRAVELING FROM			

FAVORITE THING ABOUT THE CABIN

PLACES I WOULD RECOMMEND
(RESTAURANTS, SHOPPING, ENTERTAINMENT, ETC.)

FAVORITE MEMORY FROM YOUR STAY	MESSAGE TO THE HOST

CABIN GUEST

GUEST NAME		CONTACT NUMBER	
DATE ARRIVED		DATE DEPARTED	
TRAVELING FROM			

FAVORITE THING ABOUT THE CABIN

PLACES I WOULD RECOMMEND (RESTAURANTS, SHOPPING, ENTERTAINMENT, ETC.)

FAVORITE MEMORY FROM YOUR STAY	MESSAGE TO THE HOST

CABIN GUEST

GUEST NAME		CONTACT NUMBER	
DATE ARRIVED		DATE DEPARTED	
TRAVELING FROM			

FAVORITE THING ABOUT THE CABIN

PLACES I WOULD RECOMMEND (RESTAURANTS, SHOPPING, ENTERTAINMENT, ETC.)

FAVORITE MEMORY FROM YOUR STAY	MESSAGE TO THE HOST

CABIN GUEST

GUEST NAME		CONTACT NUMBER	
DATE ARRIVED		DATE DEPARTED	
TRAVELING FROM			

FAVORITE THING ABOUT THE CABIN

PLACES I WOULD RECOMMEND
(RESTAURANTS, SHOPPING, ENTERTAINMENT, ETC.)

FAVORITE MEMORY FROM YOUR STAY	MESSAGE TO THE HOST

CABIN GUEST

GUEST NAME		CONTACT NUMBER	
DATE ARRIVED		DATE DEPARTED	
TRAVELING FROM			

FAVORITE THING ABOUT THE CABIN

PLACES I WOULD RECOMMEND
(RESTAURANTS, SHOPPING, ENTERTAINMENT, ETC.)

FAVORITE MEMORY FROM YOUR STAY	MESSAGE TO THE HOST

CABIN GUEST

GUEST NAME		CONTACT NUMBER	
DATE ARRIVED		DATE DEPARTED	
TRAVELING FROM			

FAVORITE THING ABOUT THE CABIN

PLACES I WOULD RECOMMEND
(RESTAURANTS, SHOPPING, ENTERTAINMENT, ETC.)

FAVORITE MEMORY FROM YOUR STAY	MESSAGE TO THE HOST

CABIN GUEST

GUEST NAME		CONTACT NUMBER	
DATE ARRIVED		DATE DEPARTED	
TRAVELING FROM			

FAVORITE THING ABOUT THE CABIN

PLACES I WOULD RECOMMEND
(RESTAURANTS, SHOPPING, ENTERTAINMENT, ETC.)

FAVORITE MEMORY FROM YOUR STAY	MESSAGE TO THE HOST

CABIN GUEST

GUEST NAME		CONTACT NUMBER	
DATE ARRIVED		DATE DEPARTED	
TRAVELING FROM			

FAVORITE THING ABOUT THE CABIN

PLACES I WOULD RECOMMEND (RESTAURANTS, SHOPPING, ENTERTAINMENT, ETC.)

FAVORITE MEMORY FROM YOUR STAY	MESSAGE TO THE HOST

CABIN GUEST

GUEST NAME		CONTACT NUMBER	
DATE ARRIVED		DATE DEPARTED	
TRAVELING FROM			

FAVORITE THING ABOUT THE CABIN

PLACES I WOULD RECOMMEND
(RESTAURANTS, SHOPPING, ENTERTAINMENT, ETC.)

FAVORITE MEMORY FROM YOUR STAY	MESSAGE TO THE HOST

CABIN GUEST

GUEST NAME		CONTACT NUMBER	
DATE ARRIVED		DATE DEPARTED	
TRAVELING FROM			

FAVORITE THING ABOUT THE CABIN

PLACES I WOULD RECOMMEND (RESTAURANTS, SHOPPING, ENTERTAINMENT, ETC.)

FAVORITE MEMORY FROM YOUR STAY	MESSAGE TO THE HOST

CABIN GUEST

GUEST NAME		CONTACT NUMBER	
DATE ARRIVED		DATE DEPARTED	
TRAVELING FROM			

FAVORITE THING ABOUT THE CABIN

PLACES I WOULD RECOMMEND
(RESTAURANTS, SHOPPING, ENTERTAINMENT, ETC.)

FAVORITE MEMORY FROM YOUR STAY	MESSAGE TO THE HOST

CABIN GUEST

GUEST NAME		CONTACT NUMBER	
DATE ARRIVED		DATE DEPARTED	
TRAVELING FROM			

FAVORITE THING ABOUT THE CABIN

PLACES I WOULD RECOMMEND
(RESTAURANTS, SHOPPING, ENTERTAINMENT, ETC.)

FAVORITE MEMORY FROM YOUR STAY	MESSAGE TO THE HOST

CABIN GUEST

GUEST NAME		CONTACT NUMBER	
DATE ARRIVED		DATE DEPARTED	
TRAVELING FROM			

FAVORITE THING ABOUT THE CABIN

PLACES I WOULD RECOMMEND
(RESTAURANTS, SHOPPING, ENTERTAINMENT, ETC.)

FAVORITE MEMORY FROM YOUR STAY	MESSAGE TO THE HOST

CABIN GUEST

GUEST NAME		CONTACT NUMBER	
DATE ARRIVED		DATE DEPARTED	
TRAVELING FROM			

FAVORITE THING ABOUT THE CABIN

PLACES I WOULD RECOMMEND
(RESTAURANTS, SHOPPING, ENTERTAINMENT, ETC.)

FAVORITE MEMORY FROM YOUR STAY	MESSAGE TO THE HOST

CABIN GUEST

GUEST NAME		CONTACT NUMBER	
DATE ARRIVED		DATE DEPARTED	
TRAVELING FROM			

FAVORITE THING ABOUT THE CABIN

PLACES I WOULD RECOMMEND
(RESTAURANTS, SHOPPING, ENTERTAINMENT, ETC.)

FAVORITE MEMORY FROM YOUR STAY	MESSAGE TO THE HOST

CABIN GUEST

GUEST NAME		CONTACT NUMBER	
DATE ARRIVED		DATE DEPARTED	
TRAVELING FROM			

FAVORITE THING ABOUT THE CABIN

PLACES I WOULD RECOMMEND
(RESTAURANTS, SHOPPING, ENTERTAINMENT, ETC.)

FAVORITE MEMORY FROM YOUR STAY	MESSAGE TO THE HOST

CABIN GUEST

GUEST NAME		CONTACT NUMBER	
DATE ARRIVED		DATE DEPARTED	
TRAVELING FROM			

FAVORITE THING ABOUT THE CABIN

PLACES I WOULD RECOMMEND
(RESTAURANTS, SHOPPING, ENTERTAINMENT, ETC.)

FAVORITE MEMORY FROM YOUR STAY	MESSAGE TO THE HOST

CABIN GUEST

GUEST NAME		CONTACT NUMBER	
DATE ARRIVED		DATE DEPARTED	
TRAVELING FROM			

FAVORITE THING ABOUT THE CABIN

PLACES I WOULD RECOMMEND
(RESTAURANTS, SHOPPING, ENTERTAINMENT, ETC.)

FAVORITE MEMORY FROM YOUR STAY	MESSAGE TO THE HOST

CABIN GUEST

GUEST NAME		CONTACT NUMBER	
DATE ARRIVED		DATE DEPARTED	
TRAVELING FROM			

FAVORITE THING ABOUT THE CABIN

PLACES I WOULD RECOMMEND
(RESTAURANTS, SHOPPING, ENTERTAINMENT, ETC.)

FAVORITE MEMORY FROM YOUR STAY	MESSAGE TO THE HOST

CABIN GUEST

GUEST NAME		CONTACT NUMBER	
DATE ARRIVED		DATE DEPARTED	
TRAVELING FROM			

FAVORITE THING ABOUT THE CABIN

PLACES I WOULD RECOMMEND
(RESTAURANTS, SHOPPING, ENTERTAINMENT, ETC.)

FAVORITE MEMORY FROM YOUR STAY	MESSAGE TO THE HOST

CABIN GUEST

GUEST NAME		CONTACT NUMBER	
DATE ARRIVED		DATE DEPARTED	
TRAVELING FROM			

FAVORITE THING ABOUT THE CABIN

PLACES I WOULD RECOMMEND
(RESTAURANTS, SHOPPING, ENTERTAINMENT, ETC.)

FAVORITE MEMORY FROM YOUR STAY	MESSAGE TO THE HOST

CABIN GUEST

GUEST NAME		CONTACT NUMBER	
DATE ARRIVED		DATE DEPARTED	
TRAVELING FROM			

FAVORITE THING ABOUT THE CABIN

PLACES I WOULD RECOMMEND (RESTAURANTS, SHOPPING, ENTERTAINMENT, ETC.)

FAVORITE MEMORY FROM YOUR STAY	MESSAGE TO THE HOST

CABIN GUEST

GUEST NAME		CONTACT NUMBER	
DATE ARRIVED		DATE DEPARTED	
TRAVELING FROM			

FAVORITE THING ABOUT THE CABIN

PLACES I WOULD RECOMMEND
(RESTAURANTS, SHOPPING, ENTERTAINMENT, ETC.)

FAVORITE MEMORY FROM YOUR STAY	MESSAGE TO THE HOST

CABIN GUEST

GUEST NAME		CONTACT NUMBER	
DATE ARRIVED		DATE DEPARTED	
TRAVELING FROM			

FAVORITE THING ABOUT THE CABIN

PLACES I WOULD RECOMMEND (RESTAURANTS, SHOPPING, ENTERTAINMENT, ETC.)

FAVORITE MEMORY FROM YOUR STAY	MESSAGE TO THE HOST

CABIN GUEST

GUEST NAME		CONTACT NUMBER	
DATE ARRIVED		DATE DEPARTED	
TRAVELING FROM			

FAVORITE THING ABOUT THE CABIN

PLACES I WOULD RECOMMEND
(RESTAURANTS, SHOPPING, ENTERTAINMENT, ETC.)

FAVORITE MEMORY FROM YOUR STAY	MESSAGE TO THE HOST

CABIN GUEST

GUEST NAME		CONTACT NUMBER	
DATE ARRIVED		DATE DEPARTED	
TRAVELING FROM			

FAVORITE THING ABOUT THE CABIN

PLACES I WOULD RECOMMEND (RESTAURANTS, SHOPPING, ENTERTAINMENT, ETC.)

FAVORITE MEMORY FROM YOUR STAY	MESSAGE TO THE HOST

CABIN GUEST

GUEST NAME		CONTACT NUMBER	
DATE ARRIVED		DATE DEPARTED	
TRAVELING FROM			

FAVORITE THING ABOUT THE CABIN

PLACES I WOULD RECOMMEND
(RESTAURANTS, SHOPPING, ENTERTAINMENT, ETC.)

FAVORITE MEMORY FROM YOUR STAY	MESSAGE TO THE HOST

CABIN GUEST

GUEST NAME		CONTACT NUMBER	
DATE ARRIVED		DATE DEPARTED	
TRAVELING FROM			

FAVORITE THING ABOUT THE CABIN

PLACES I WOULD RECOMMEND
(RESTAURANTS, SHOPPING, ENTERTAINMENT, ETC.)

FAVORITE MEMORY FROM YOUR STAY	MESSAGE TO THE HOST

CABIN GUEST

GUEST NAME		CONTACT NUMBER	
DATE ARRIVED		DATE DEPARTED	
TRAVELING FROM			

FAVORITE THING ABOUT THE CABIN

PLACES I WOULD RECOMMEND
(RESTAURANTS, SHOPPING, ENTERTAINMENT, ETC.)

FAVORITE MEMORY FROM YOUR STAY	MESSAGE TO THE HOST

CABIN GUEST

GUEST NAME		CONTACT NUMBER	
DATE ARRIVED		DATE DEPARTED	
TRAVELING FROM			

FAVORITE THING ABOUT THE CABIN

PLACES I WOULD RECOMMEND
(RESTAURANTS, SHOPPING, ENTERTAINMENT, ETC.)

FAVORITE MEMORY FROM YOUR STAY	MESSAGE TO THE HOST

CABIN GUEST

GUEST NAME		CONTACT NUMBER	
DATE ARRIVED		DATE DEPARTED	
TRAVELING FROM			

FAVORITE THING ABOUT THE CABIN

PLACES I WOULD RECOMMEND
(RESTAURANTS, SHOPPING, ENTERTAINMENT, ETC.)

FAVORITE MEMORY FROM YOUR STAY	MESSAGE TO THE HOST

CABIN GUEST

GUEST NAME		CONTACT NUMBER	
DATE ARRIVED		DATE DEPARTED	
TRAVELING FROM			

FAVORITE THING ABOUT THE CABIN

PLACES I WOULD RECOMMEND
(RESTAURANTS, SHOPPING, ENTERTAINMENT, ETC.)

FAVORITE MEMORY FROM YOUR STAY	MESSAGE TO THE HOST

CABIN GUEST

GUEST NAME		CONTACT NUMBER	
DATE ARRIVED		DATE DEPARTED	
TRAVELING FROM			

FAVORITE THING ABOUT THE CABIN

PLACES I WOULD RECOMMEND
(RESTAURANTS, SHOPPING, ENTERTAINMENT, ETC.)

FAVORITE MEMORY FROM YOUR STAY	MESSAGE TO THE HOST

CABIN GUEST

GUEST NAME		CONTACT NUMBER	
DATE ARRIVED		DATE DEPARTED	
TRAVELING FROM			

FAVORITE THING ABOUT THE CABIN

PLACES I WOULD RECOMMEND (RESTAURANTS, SHOPPING, ENTERTAINMENT, ETC.)

FAVORITE MEMORY FROM YOUR STAY	MESSAGE TO THE HOST

CABIN GUEST

GUEST NAME		CONTACT NUMBER	
DATE ARRIVED		DATE DEPARTED	
TRAVELING FROM			

FAVORITE THING ABOUT THE CABIN

PLACES I WOULD RECOMMEND (RESTAURANTS, SHOPPING, ENTERTAINMENT, ETC.)

FAVORITE MEMORY FROM YOUR STAY	MESSAGE TO THE HOST

CABIN GUEST

GUEST NAME		CONTACT NUMBER	
DATE ARRIVED		DATE DEPARTED	
TRAVELING FROM			

FAVORITE THING ABOUT THE CABIN

PLACES I WOULD RECOMMEND
(RESTAURANTS, SHOPPING, ENTERTAINMENT, ETC.)

FAVORITE MEMORY FROM YOUR STAY	MESSAGE TO THE HOST

CABIN GUEST

GUEST NAME		CONTACT NUMBER	
DATE ARRIVED		DATE DEPARTED	
TRAVELING FROM			

FAVORITE THING ABOUT THE CABIN

PLACES I WOULD RECOMMEND (RESTAURANTS, SHOPPING, ENTERTAINMENT, ETC.)

FAVORITE MEMORY FROM YOUR STAY	MESSAGE TO THE HOST

CABIN GUEST

GUEST NAME		CONTACT NUMBER	
DATE ARRIVED		DATE DEPARTED	
TRAVELING FROM			

FAVORITE THING ABOUT THE CABIN

PLACES I WOULD RECOMMEND (RESTAURANTS, SHOPPING, ENTERTAINMENT, ETC.)

FAVORITE MEMORY FROM YOUR STAY	MESSAGE TO THE HOST

CABIN GUEST

GUEST NAME		CONTACT NUMBER	
DATE ARRIVED		DATE DEPARTED	
TRAVELING FROM			

FAVORITE THING ABOUT THE CABIN

PLACES I WOULD RECOMMEND
(RESTAURANTS, SHOPPING, ENTERTAINMENT, ETC.)

FAVORITE MEMORY FROM YOUR STAY	MESSAGE TO THE HOST

CABIN GUEST

GUEST NAME		CONTACT NUMBER	
DATE ARRIVED		DATE DEPARTED	
TRAVELING FROM			

FAVORITE THING ABOUT THE CABIN

PLACES I WOULD RECOMMEND (RESTAURANTS, SHOPPING, ENTERTAINMENT, ETC.)

FAVORITE MEMORY FROM YOUR STAY	MESSAGE TO THE HOST

CABIN GUEST

GUEST NAME		CONTACT NUMBER	
DATE ARRIVED		DATE DEPARTED	
TRAVELING FROM			

FAVORITE THING ABOUT THE CABIN

PLACES I WOULD RECOMMEND
(RESTAURANTS, SHOPPING, ENTERTAINMENT, ETC.)

FAVORITE MEMORY FROM YOUR STAY	MESSAGE TO THE HOST

CABIN GUEST

GUEST NAME		CONTACT NUMBER	
DATE ARRIVED		DATE DEPARTED	
TRAVELING FROM			

FAVORITE THING ABOUT THE CABIN

PLACES I WOULD RECOMMEND (RESTAURANTS, SHOPPING, ENTERTAINMENT, ETC.)

FAVORITE MEMORY FROM YOUR STAY	MESSAGE TO THE HOST

CABIN GUEST

GUEST NAME		CONTACT NUMBER	
DATE ARRIVED		DATE DEPARTED	
TRAVELING FROM			

FAVORITE THING ABOUT THE CABIN

PLACES I WOULD RECOMMEND
(RESTAURANTS, SHOPPING, ENTERTAINMENT, ETC.)

FAVORITE MEMORY FROM YOUR STAY	MESSAGE TO THE HOST

CABIN GUEST

GUEST NAME		CONTACT NUMBER	
DATE ARRIVED		DATE DEPARTED	
TRAVELING FROM			

FAVORITE THING ABOUT THE CABIN

PLACES I WOULD RECOMMEND (RESTAURANTS, SHOPPING, ENTERTAINMENT, ETC.)

FAVORITE MEMORY FROM YOUR STAY	MESSAGE TO THE HOST

CABIN GUEST

GUEST NAME		CONTACT NUMBER	
DATE ARRIVED		DATE DEPARTED	
TRAVELING FROM			

FAVORITE THING ABOUT THE CABIN

PLACES I WOULD RECOMMEND
(RESTAURANTS, SHOPPING, ENTERTAINMENT, ETC.)

FAVORITE MEMORY FROM YOUR STAY	MESSAGE TO THE HOST

CABIN GUEST

GUEST NAME		CONTACT NUMBER	
DATE ARRIVED		DATE DEPARTED	
TRAVELING FROM			

FAVORITE THING ABOUT THE CABIN

PLACES I WOULD RECOMMEND (RESTAURANTS, SHOPPING, ENTERTAINMENT, ETC.)

FAVORITE MEMORY FROM YOUR STAY	MESSAGE TO THE HOST

CABIN GUEST

GUEST NAME		CONTACT NUMBER	
DATE ARRIVED		DATE DEPARTED	
TRAVELING FROM			

FAVORITE THING ABOUT THE CABIN

PLACES I WOULD RECOMMEND
(RESTAURANTS, SHOPPING, ENTERTAINMENT, ETC.)

FAVORITE MEMORY FROM YOUR STAY	MESSAGE TO THE HOST

CABIN GUEST

GUEST NAME		CONTACT NUMBER	
DATE ARRIVED		DATE DEPARTED	
TRAVELING FROM			

FAVORITE THING ABOUT THE CABIN

PLACES I WOULD RECOMMEND (RESTAURANTS, SHOPPING, ENTERTAINMENT, ETC.)

FAVORITE MEMORY FROM YOUR STAY	MESSAGE TO THE HOST

CABIN GUEST

GUEST NAME		CONTACT NUMBER	
DATE ARRIVED		DATE DEPARTED	
TRAVELING FROM			

FAVORITE THING ABOUT THE CABIN

PLACES I WOULD RECOMMEND
(RESTAURANTS, SHOPPING, ENTERTAINMENT, ETC.)

FAVORITE MEMORY FROM YOUR STAY	MESSAGE TO THE HOST

CABIN GUEST

GUEST NAME		CONTACT NUMBER	
DATE ARRIVED		DATE DEPARTED	
TRAVELING FROM			

FAVORITE THING ABOUT THE CABIN

PLACES I WOULD RECOMMEND
(RESTAURANTS, SHOPPING, ENTERTAINMENT, ETC.)

FAVORITE MEMORY FROM YOUR STAY	MESSAGE TO THE HOST

CABIN GUEST

GUEST NAME		CONTACT NUMBER	
DATE ARRIVED		DATE DEPARTED	
TRAVELING FROM			

FAVORITE THING ABOUT THE CABIN

PLACES I WOULD RECOMMEND
(RESTAURANTS, SHOPPING, ENTERTAINMENT, ETC.)

FAVORITE MEMORY FROM YOUR STAY	MESSAGE TO THE HOST

CABIN GUEST

GUEST NAME		CONTACT NUMBER	
DATE ARRIVED		DATE DEPARTED	
TRAVELING FROM			

FAVORITE THING ABOUT THE CABIN

PLACES I WOULD RECOMMEND
(RESTAURANTS, SHOPPING, ENTERTAINMENT, ETC.)

FAVORITE MEMORY FROM YOUR STAY	MESSAGE TO THE HOST

CABIN GUEST

GUEST NAME		CONTACT NUMBER	
DATE ARRIVED		DATE DEPARTED	
TRAVELING FROM			

FAVORITE THING ABOUT THE CABIN

PLACES I WOULD RECOMMEND
(RESTAURANTS, SHOPPING, ENTERTAINMENT, ETC.)

FAVORITE MEMORY FROM YOUR STAY	MESSAGE TO THE HOST

CABIN GUEST

GUEST NAME		CONTACT NUMBER	
DATE ARRIVED		DATE DEPARTED	
TRAVELING FROM			

FAVORITE THING ABOUT THE CABIN

PLACES I WOULD RECOMMEND (RESTAURANTS, SHOPPING, ENTERTAINMENT, ETC.)

FAVORITE MEMORY FROM YOUR STAY	MESSAGE TO THE HOST

CABIN GUEST

GUEST NAME		CONTACT NUMBER	
DATE ARRIVED		DATE DEPARTED	
TRAVELING FROM			

FAVORITE THING ABOUT THE CABIN

PLACES I WOULD RECOMMEND
(RESTAURANTS, SHOPPING, ENTERTAINMENT, ETC.)

FAVORITE MEMORY FROM YOUR STAY	MESSAGE TO THE HOST

CABIN GUEST

GUEST NAME		CONTACT NUMBER	
DATE ARRIVED		DATE DEPARTED	
TRAVELING FROM			

FAVORITE THING ABOUT THE CABIN

PLACES I WOULD RECOMMEND
(RESTAURANTS, SHOPPING, ENTERTAINMENT, ETC.)

FAVORITE MEMORY FROM YOUR STAY	MESSAGE TO THE HOST

CABIN GUEST

GUEST NAME		CONTACT NUMBER	
DATE ARRIVED		DATE DEPARTED	
TRAVELING FROM			

FAVORITE THING ABOUT THE CABIN

PLACES I WOULD RECOMMEND (RESTAURANTS, SHOPPING, ENTERTAINMENT, ETC.)

FAVORITE MEMORY FROM YOUR STAY	MESSAGE TO THE HOST

CABIN GUEST

GUEST NAME		CONTACT NUMBER	
DATE ARRIVED		DATE DEPARTED	
TRAVELING FROM			

FAVORITE THING ABOUT THE CABIN

PLACES I WOULD RECOMMEND (RESTAURANTS, SHOPPING, ENTERTAINMENT, ETC.)

FAVORITE MEMORY FROM YOUR STAY	MESSAGE TO THE HOST

CABIN GUEST

GUEST NAME		CONTACT NUMBER	
DATE ARRIVED		DATE DEPARTED	
TRAVELING FROM			

FAVORITE THING ABOUT THE CABIN

PLACES I WOULD RECOMMEND
(RESTAURANTS, SHOPPING, ENTERTAINMENT, ETC.)

FAVORITE MEMORY FROM YOUR STAY	MESSAGE TO THE HOST

CABIN GUEST

GUEST NAME		CONTACT NUMBER	
DATE ARRIVED		DATE DEPARTED	
TRAVELING FROM			

FAVORITE THING ABOUT THE CABIN

PLACES I WOULD RECOMMEND
(RESTAURANTS, SHOPPING, ENTERTAINMENT, ETC.)

FAVORITE MEMORY FROM YOUR STAY	MESSAGE TO THE HOST

CABIN GUEST

GUEST NAME		CONTACT NUMBER	
DATE ARRIVED		DATE DEPARTED	
TRAVELING FROM			

FAVORITE THING ABOUT THE CABIN

PLACES I WOULD RECOMMEND
(RESTAURANTS, SHOPPING, ENTERTAINMENT, ETC.)

FAVORITE MEMORY FROM YOUR STAY	MESSAGE TO THE HOST

CABIN GUEST

GUEST NAME		CONTACT NUMBER	
DATE ARRIVED		DATE DEPARTED	
TRAVELING FROM			

FAVORITE THING ABOUT THE CABIN

PLACES I WOULD RECOMMEND (RESTAURANTS, SHOPPING, ENTERTAINMENT, ETC.)

FAVORITE MEMORY FROM YOUR STAY	MESSAGE TO THE HOST

CABIN GUEST

GUEST NAME		CONTACT NUMBER	
DATE ARRIVED		DATE DEPARTED	
TRAVELING FROM			

FAVORITE THING ABOUT THE CABIN

PLACES I WOULD RECOMMEND
(RESTAURANTS, SHOPPING, ENTERTAINMENT, ETC.)

FAVORITE MEMORY FROM YOUR STAY	MESSAGE TO THE HOST

CABIN GUEST

GUEST NAME		CONTACT NUMBER	
DATE ARRIVED		DATE DEPARTED	
TRAVELING FROM			

FAVORITE THING ABOUT THE CABIN

PLACES I WOULD RECOMMEND (RESTAURANTS, SHOPPING, ENTERTAINMENT, ETC.)

FAVORITE MEMORY FROM YOUR STAY	MESSAGE TO THE HOST

CABIN GUEST

GUEST NAME		CONTACT NUMBER	
DATE ARRIVED		DATE DEPARTED	
TRAVELING FROM			

FAVORITE THING ABOUT THE CABIN

PLACES I WOULD RECOMMEND
(RESTAURANTS, SHOPPING, ENTERTAINMENT, ETC.)

FAVORITE MEMORY FROM YOUR STAY	MESSAGE TO THE HOST

CABIN GUEST

GUEST NAME		CONTACT NUMBER	
DATE ARRIVED		DATE DEPARTED	
TRAVELING FROM			

FAVORITE THING ABOUT THE CABIN

PLACES I WOULD RECOMMEND (RESTAURANTS, SHOPPING, ENTERTAINMENT, ETC.)

FAVORITE MEMORY FROM YOUR STAY	MESSAGE TO THE HOST

CABIN GUEST

GUEST NAME		CONTACT NUMBER	
DATE ARRIVED		DATE DEPARTED	
TRAVELING FROM			

FAVORITE THING ABOUT THE CABIN

PLACES I WOULD RECOMMEND
(RESTAURANTS, SHOPPING, ENTERTAINMENT, ETC.)

FAVORITE MEMORY FROM YOUR STAY	MESSAGE TO THE HOST

CABIN GUEST

GUEST NAME		CONTACT NUMBER	
DATE ARRIVED		DATE DEPARTED	
TRAVELING FROM			

FAVORITE THING ABOUT THE CABIN

PLACES I WOULD RECOMMEND (RESTAURANTS, SHOPPING, ENTERTAINMENT, ETC.)

FAVORITE MEMORY FROM YOUR STAY	MESSAGE TO THE HOST

CABIN GUEST

GUEST NAME		CONTACT NUMBER	
DATE ARRIVED		DATE DEPARTED	
TRAVELING FROM			

FAVORITE THING ABOUT THE CABIN

PLACES I WOULD RECOMMEND
(RESTAURANTS, SHOPPING, ENTERTAINMENT, ETC.)

FAVORITE MEMORY FROM YOUR STAY	MESSAGE TO THE HOST

CABIN GUEST

GUEST NAME		CONTACT NUMBER	
DATE ARRIVED		DATE DEPARTED	
TRAVELING FROM			

FAVORITE THING ABOUT THE CABIN

PLACES I WOULD RECOMMEND
(RESTAURANTS, SHOPPING, ENTERTAINMENT, ETC.)

FAVORITE MEMORY FROM YOUR STAY	MESSAGE TO THE HOST

CABIN GUEST

GUEST NAME		CONTACT NUMBER	
DATE ARRIVED		DATE DEPARTED	
TRAVELING FROM			

FAVORITE THING ABOUT THE CABIN

PLACES I WOULD RECOMMEND
(RESTAURANTS, SHOPPING, ENTERTAINMENT, ETC.)

FAVORITE MEMORY FROM YOUR STAY	MESSAGE TO THE HOST

CABIN GUEST

GUEST NAME		CONTACT NUMBER	
DATE ARRIVED		DATE DEPARTED	
TRAVELING FROM			

FAVORITE THING ABOUT THE CABIN

PLACES I WOULD RECOMMEND (RESTAURANTS, SHOPPING, ENTERTAINMENT, ETC.)

FAVORITE MEMORY FROM YOUR STAY	MESSAGE TO THE HOST

CABIN GUEST

GUEST NAME		CONTACT NUMBER	
DATE ARRIVED		DATE DEPARTED	
TRAVELING FROM			

FAVORITE THING ABOUT THE CABIN

PLACES I WOULD RECOMMEND
(RESTAURANTS, SHOPPING, ENTERTAINMENT, ETC.)

FAVORITE MEMORY FROM YOUR STAY	MESSAGE TO THE HOST

CABIN GUEST

GUEST NAME		CONTACT NUMBER	
DATE ARRIVED		DATE DEPARTED	
TRAVELING FROM			

FAVORITE THING ABOUT THE CABIN

PLACES I WOULD RECOMMEND (RESTAURANTS, SHOPPING, ENTERTAINMENT, ETC.)

FAVORITE MEMORY FROM YOUR STAY	MESSAGE TO THE HOST

www.ingramcontent.com/pod-product-compliance
Lightning Source LLC
Chambersburg PA
CBHW081232080526
44587CB00022B/3920